# GATE TEST PREP GUIDE

## Critical thinking tests for Grade 2 to 5

### Practice tests for COGAT
### Gifted and Talented Education

Edition 1

By

Divyanshi Suri

# INTRODUCTION

Welcome to the world of critical thinking and problem solving !!
Is your child going to take GATE test this year or you want to improve your child's
thinking skills?

Here is a complete solution, which covers most of the patterns and tests the critical
thinking from various angles.

Let's  first understand GATE
**GATE stands for Gifted and Talented Education**
The GATE test is used by many public school districts including several in California
and New York State. It is an IQ test for kids based upon the Otis-Lennon School
Ability Test (OLSAT). The tests measure basic math, reasoning and
verbal/non-verbal  skills and are typically given in the 3rd through 5th grades. This
book has been designed after studying actual tests and using their methodologies.
It is geared toward the GATE, NNAT and the OLSAT test, SCAT, NYC G&T.

The book contains 7 different topics in which children will be able to learn different
things. These topics are Identifying Shapes, Relating and Connecting Ideas,
Completing Patterns, Picture Analogies, Finding Differences etc.

The NNAT measures nonverbal reasoning and problem solving skills. It has 4
categories of questions are pattern completion, reasoning by analogy, serial
reasoning and spatial visualization. The NNAT is designed to measure nonverbal
reasoning skills without the use of language. Children will be tested on their
problem solving abilities and to demonstrate an understanding of relationships.

This books is a great resource for students who are planning to appear for the
CogAT test in Grade 2 . It also includes useful tips for preparing for the CogAT test.
It has one full length test similar in format to the actual test that will be
administered in the CogAT Test.

It is a 35 full color paged children's test prep workbook for gifted and talented
training from ages 5-9.

**"Do not train a child to learn by force or harshness; but direct them to it by what
amuses their minds, so that you may be better able to discover with accuracy the
peculiar bent of the genius of each."**
**- Plato**

# ABOUT THE AUTHOR

Divyanshi is a high school Junior, passionate about learning new things, and creating educational content for elementary school students. Aspiring be an engineer, she finds a great interest in helping students, in understanding different academic concepts from mathematics to any STEM topics.

While teaching her twin brothers for the GATE test, she got an idea to put all the examples together and create a GATE book. The idea was to help all the elementary school kids, to prepare for the cognitive tests.

Other than creating study material, she created some cool iPhone and Android educational Apps.  In addition to book writing and app creation, she enjoys dancing and cooking. She also does a lot of volunteering activities, to help the underprivileged children.


*"In learning you will teach, and in teaching you will learn"*
- Phil Collins

# CONTENTS

In the following questions, identify the figure that completes the pattern

**1.**

X   (1)   (2)   (3)   (4)

| A: 1 | B: 2 |
|------|------|
| C: 3 | D: 4 |

**2.**

X   (1)   (2)   (3)  (4)

| A: 1 | B: 2 |
|------|------|
| C: 3 | D: 4 |

**3.**

X   (1)   (2)   (3)  (4)

| A: 1 | B: 2 |
|------|------|
| C: 3 | D: 4 |

**4.**

X       (1)      (2)      (3)      (4)

| A: 1 | B: 2 |
|------|------|
| C: 3 | D: 4 |

**5.**           

X       (1)      (2)      (3)      (4)

| A: 1 | B: 2 |
|------|------|
| C: 3 | D: 4 |

**6.**      

X       (1)      (2)      (3)      (4)

| A: 1 | B: 2 |
|------|------|
| C: 3 | D: 4 |

**7.**             

X       (1)      (2)      (3)      (4)

| A: 1 | B: 2 |
|------|------|
| C: 3 | D: 4 |

**8.**

X          (1)          (2)          (3)          (4)

| A: 1 | B: 2 |
|------|------|
| C: 3 | D: 4 |

**9.**

X          (1)          (2)          (3)          (4)

| A: 1 | B: 2 |
|------|------|
| C: 3 | D: 4 |

**10.**

X          (1)          (2)          (3)          (4)

| A: 1 | B: 2 |
|------|------|
| C: 3 | D: 4 |

# UNIT 2 : SERIAL REASONING

Select a figure from amongst the Answer Figures which will continue the same series as established by the five Problem Figures.

**1.**

Answer figures

| □△○ | ○ 0 × | ×△ 0 | 0 △ ↑ | ↑ △△ | | △ ○ $ | $ ○ ↑ | △ ○ $ | △ ↑ N | △ ↑ □ |
|---|---|---|---|---|---|---|---|---|---|---|
| C △ 0 | △△ C | ★ ○△ | ○△ ★ | ↑ 0 ○ | | 0 △ ↑ | 0 △ ↑ | 0 △ N | ○△ 0 | ○△ 0 |
| A | B | C | D | E | | 1 | 2 | 3 | 4 | 5 |

| | |
|---|---|
| A:  1 | B:  2 |
| C:  3 | D:  4 |
| E:  5 | |

**2.**

Answer figures

| A | B | C | D | E | | 1 | 2 | 3 | 4 | 5 |
|---|---|---|---|---|---|---|---|---|---|---|

| | |
|---|---|
| A:  1 | B:  2 |
| C:  3 | D:  4 |
| E:  5 | |

**3.**

Answer figures

| A | B | C | D | E | | 1 | 2 | 3 | 4 | 5 |
|---|---|---|---|---|---|---|---|---|---|---|

| | |
|---|---|
| A:  1 | B:  2 |
| C:  3 | D:  4 |
| E:  5 | |

**4.**

Answer figures

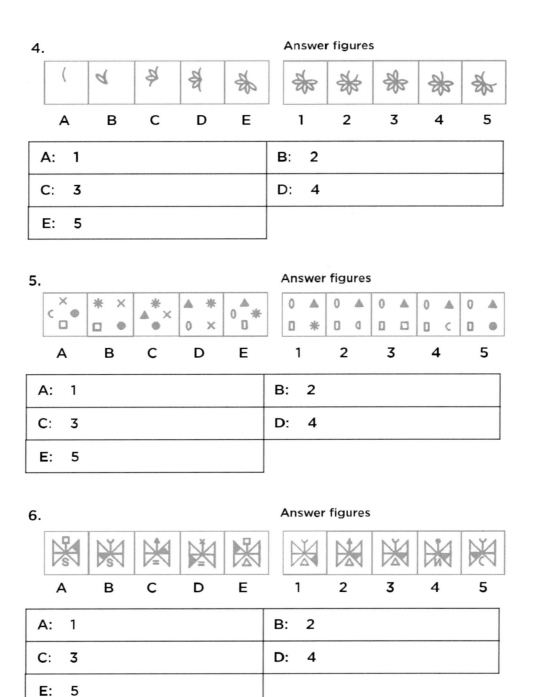

| A | B | C | D | E | 1 | 2 | 3 | 4 | 5 |

| A: | 1 | B: | 2 |
|---|---|---|---|
| C: | 3 | D: | 4 |
| E: | 5 | | |

**5.**

Answer figures

| A | B | C | D | E | 1 | 2 | 3 | 4 | 5 |

| A: | 1 | B: | 2 |
|---|---|---|---|
| C: | 3 | D: | 4 |
| E: | 5 | | |

**6.**

Answer figures

| A | B | C | D | E | 1 | 2 | 3 | 4 | 5 |

| A: | 1 | B: | 2 |
|---|---|---|---|
| C: | 3 | D: | 4 |
| E: | 5 | | |

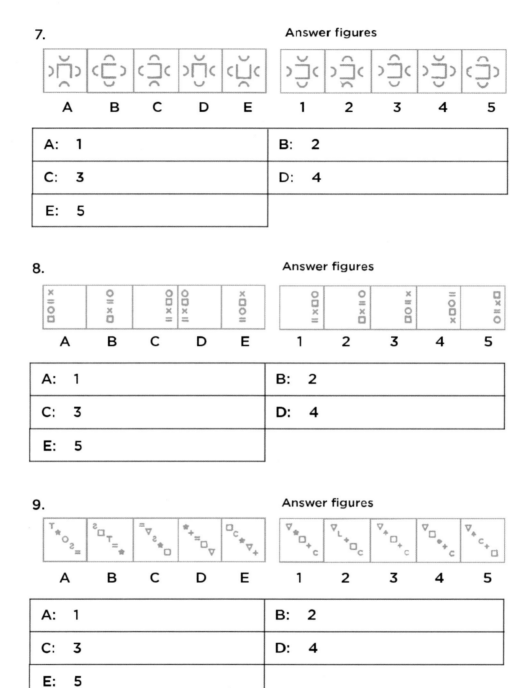

**7.** Answer figures

| A | B | C | D | E |
|---|---|---|---|---|

| 1 | 2 | 3 | 4 | 5 |
|---|---|---|---|---|

| A: 1 | B: 2 |
|---|---|
| C: 3 | D: 4 |
| E: 5 | |

**8.** Answer figures

| A | B | C | D | E |
|---|---|---|---|---|

| 1 | 2 | 3 | 4 | 5 |
|---|---|---|---|---|

| A: 1 | B: 2 |
|---|---|
| C: 3 | D: 4 |
| E: 5 | |

**9.** Answer figures

| A | B | C | D | E |
|---|---|---|---|---|

| 1 | 2 | 3 | 4 | 5 |
|---|---|---|---|---|

| A: 1 | B: 2 |
|---|---|
| C: 3 | D: 4 |
| E: 5 | |

**10.**

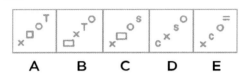

| A | B | C | D | E | | 1 | 2 | 3 | 4 | 5 |

| A: | 1 | B: | 2 |
|---|---|---|---|
| C: | 3 | D: | 4 |
| E: | 5 | | |

# UNIT 3 : SPATIAL VISUALIZATION

Choose the alternative which is closely resembles the mirror image of the given combination.

**1.**

247596         695742    ઘટτⱯՏ    ઘટτⱯՏ    ઘટτⱯՏ

     X            (1)     (2)     (3)     (4)

| A: | 1 | B: | 2 |
|----|---|----|---|
| C: | 3 | D: | 4 |

**2.**

     X          (1)     (2)     (3)     (4)

| A: | 1 | B: | 2 |
|----|---|----|---|
| C: | 3 | D: | 4 |

**3.**

     X          (1)     (2)     (3)     (4)

| A: | 1 | B: | 2 |
|----|---|----|---|
| C: | 3 | D: | 4 |

**4.**

X        (1)        (2)        (3)        (4)

| A: 1 | B: 2 |
|------|------|
| C: 3 | D: 4 |

**5.**

X        (1)        (2)        (3)        (4)

| A: 1 | B: 2 |
|------|------|
| C: 3 | D: 4 |

**6.**

X        (1)        (2)        (3)        (4)

| A: 1 | B: 2 |
|------|------|
| C: 3 | D: 4 |

**7. Choose a figure which would most closely resemble the unfolded form of Figure (Z).**

X   Y   Z      (1)      (2)      (3)      (4)

| A: 1 | B: 2 |
|------|------|
| C: 3 | D: 4 |

**8. Choose a figure which would most closely resemble the unfolded form of Figure (Z).**

X     Y     Z

(1)     (2)     (3)     (4)

| A: 1 | B: 2 |
|------|------|
| C: 3 | D: 4 |

**9.**

X     Y     Z

(1)     (2)     (3)     (4)

| A: 1 | B: 2 |
|------|------|
| C: 3 | D: 4 |

**10.**

X

(1)     (2)     (3)     (4)

| A: 1 | B: 2 |
|------|------|
| C: 3 | D: 4 |

Select a suitable figure from the four alternatives that would complete the figure matrix.

1.

   X  (1)  (2)  (3)  (4)

| A: 1 | B: 2 |
|---|---|
| C: 3 | D: 4 |

2.

   X  (1)  (2)  (3)  (4)

| A: 1 | B: 2 |
|---|---|
| C: 3 | D: 4 |

3.

   X  (1)  (2)  (3)  (4)

| A: 1 | B: 2 |
|---|---|
| C: 3 | D: 4 |

**4.**

X

(1)

(2)

(3)

(4)

| A: | 1 | B: | 2 |
|----|---|----|---|
| C: | 3 | D: | 4 |

**5.**

?

X

(1)  (2)  (3)  (4)

| A: | 1 | B: | 2 |
|----|---|----|---|
| C: | 3 | D: | 4 |

**6.**

X

(1)

(2)

(3)

(4)

| A: | 1 | B: | 2 |
|----|---|----|---|
| C: | 3 | D: | 4 |

**7.**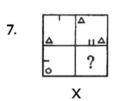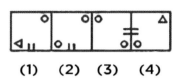

X          (1)   (2)   (3)   (4)

| A: | 1 | B: | 2 |
|---|---|---|---|
| C: | 3 | D: | 4 |

**8.**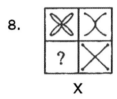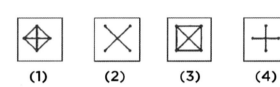

X          (1)       (2)       (3)       (4)

| A: | 1 | B: | 2 |
|---|---|---|---|
| C: | 3 | D: | 4 |

**9.**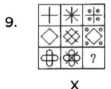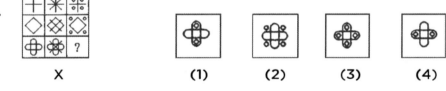

X          (1)       (2)       (3)       (4)

| A: | 1 | B: | 2 |
|---|---|---|---|
| C: | 3 | D: | 4 |

10.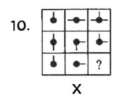

X

(1)　　　　(2)　　　　(3)　　　　(4)

| A: | 1 | B: | 2 |
|----|---|----|---|
| C: | 3 | D: | 4 |

17

Select a suitable figure from the Answer Figures that would replace the question mark (?).

1.

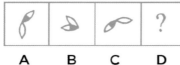

Answer figures

| A: | 1 | B: | 2 |
|---|---|---|---|
| C: | 3 | D: | 4 |
| E: | 5 | | |

2.

Answer figures

| A: | 1 | B: | 2 |
|---|---|---|---|
| C: | 3 | D: | 4 |
| E: | 5 | | |

3.

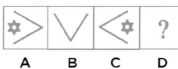

Answer figures

| A: | 1 | B: | 2 |
|---|---|---|---|
| C: | 3 | D: | 4 |
| E: | 5 | | |

Select a suitable figure from the Answer Figures that would replace the question mark (?).

**4.**

Answer figures

| A | B | C | D |
|---|---|---|---|

| 1 | 2 | 3 | 4 | 5 |
|---|---|---|---|---|

| A: 1 | B: 2 |
|------|------|
| C: 3 | D: 4 |
| E: 5 | |

**5.**

Answer figures

| A | B | C | D |
|---|---|---|---|

| 1 | 2 | 3 | 4 | 5 |
|---|---|---|---|---|

| A: 1 | B: 2 |
|------|------|
| C: 3 | D: 4 |
| E: 5 | |

**6.**

Answer figures

| A | B | C | D |
|---|---|---|---|

| 1 | 2 | 3 | 4 | 5 |
|---|---|---|---|---|

| A: 1 | B: 2 |
|------|------|
| C: 3 | D: 4 |
| E: 5 | |

Select a suitable figure from the Answer Figures that would replace the question mark (?).

**7.**

A  B  C  D

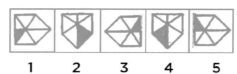

1  2  3  4  5

| A: 1 | B: 2 |
|------|------|
| C: 3 | D: 4 |
| E: 5 | |

**8.**

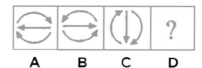

A  B  C  D

Answer figures

1  2  3  4  5

| A: 1 | B: 2 |
|------|------|
| C: 3 | D: 4 |
| E: 5 | |

**9.**

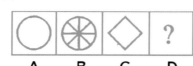

A  B  C  D

Answer figures

1  2  3  4  5

| A: 1 | B: 2 |
|------|------|
| C: 3 | D: 4 |
| E: 5 | |

Select a suitable figure from the Answer Figures that would replace the question mark (?).

10.

A   B   C   D

1   2   3   4   5

| A: 1 | B: 2 |
|------|------|
| C: 3 | D: 4 |
| E: 5 | |

# UNIT 6: LOGICAL THINKING

Look at the picture below and answer the questions given in the table

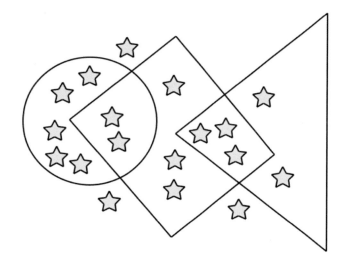

| | |
|---|---|
| Number of Stars, only in the circle | |
| Number of Stars, only in the square | |
| Number of Stars, only in the triangle | |
| Number of Stars, in both circle and the square | |
| Number of Stars, in both square and the triangle | |
| Number of Stars, in neither the circle nor the triangle | |
| Number of Stars, not in any of the shapes<br>Total number of Stars | |

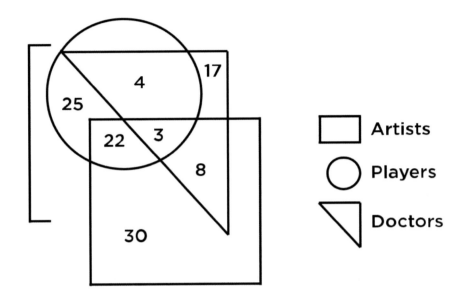

| | |
|---|---|
| How many doctors are neither artists nor players ? | |
| How many doctors are both players and artists ? | |
| How many artists are players ? | |
| How many players are neither artists nor doctors ? | |
| How many artists are neither players nor doctors ? | |

23

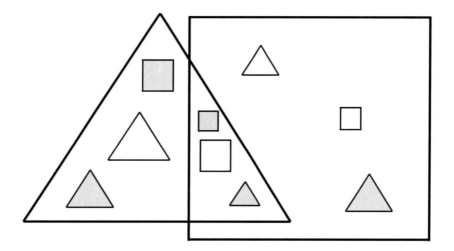

| | |
|---|---|
| Triangles in big triangle | |
| Squares in big squares | |
| Triangles in big triangle only | |
| Squares in big squares only | |
| Squares in both big shapes | |
| Triangles in both big shapes | |
| Triangles in Big square only | |
| Squares in big triangle only | |

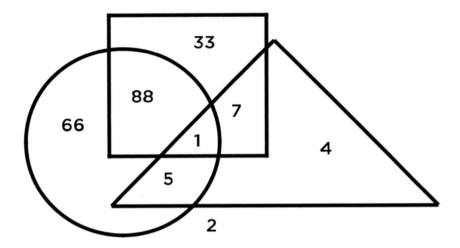

Which numbers are in either triangle or the square

Which numbers are in both the triangle and the square

Which numbers are in both the square and the circle

Which numbers are in either circle or the triangle

Which numbers are in all the three shapes

Which numbers are not in any shape

Which numbers are in neither the circle, not the triangle

Which numbers are in neither the circle nor the square

| ♡ | ♡ | | ♡ | |
|---|---|---|---|---|
| ♡ | | ♡ | | ♡ |
| ♡ | ♡ | | ♡ | |
| | | ♡ | | ♡ |

| | |
|---|---|
| How many hearts are not in the top row? | |
| How many hearts are not in the bottom row? | |
| How many hearts are not in the middle two rows? | |
| How many hearts are not in the top two rows? | |
| How many hearts are there in all? | |
| How many blank spaces are there in all? | |

In the following problems, choose the odd image out, which is different from the rest images.

1.

| A: | 1 | B: | 2 |
|----|---|----|---|
| C: | 3 | D: | 4 |
| E: | 5 | | |

2.

| A: | 1 | B: | 2 |
|----|---|----|---|
| C: | 3 | D: | 4 |
| E: | 5 | | |

3.

| A: | 1 | B: | 2 |
|----|---|----|---|
| C: | 3 | D: | 4 |
| E: | 5 | | |

**4.**

| A: | 1 | B: | 2 |
|---|---|---|---|
| C: | 3 | D: | 4 |
| E: | 5 | | |

**5.**

| A: | 1 | B: | 2 |
|---|---|---|---|
| C: | 3 | D: | 4 |
| E: | 5 | | |

**6.**

| A: | 1 | B: | 2 |
|---|---|---|---|
| C: | 3 | D: | 4 |
| E: | 5 | | |

**7.**

| A: | 1 | B: | 2 |
|---|---|---|---|
| C: | 3 | D: | 4 |
| E: | 5 | | |

**8.**

| A: | 1 | B: | 2 |
|----|---|----|---|
| C: | 3 | D: | 4 |
| E: | 5 | | |

**9.**

| A: | 1 | B: | 2 |
|----|---|----|---|
| C: | 3 | D: | 4 |
| E: | 5 | | |

**10.**

| A: | 1 | B: | 2 |
|----|---|----|---|
| C: | 3 | D: | 4 |
| E: | 5 | | |

In the following problems, choose the odd image out, which is different from the rest images.

1.
Fact 1: All boys like to run.
Fact 2: Some boys like to swim.
Fact 3: Some boys look like their dads.

If the first three statements are facts, which of the following statements must also be a fact?
I: All boys who like to swim look like their dads.
II: boys who like to swim also like to run.
III: boys who like to run do not look like their dads.

| A: | I only | B: | II only |
|---|---|---|---|
| C: | II and III only | D: | None of the statements is a known fact. |

2.
Fact 1: Martha has four children
Fact 2: Two of the children have blue eyes and two of the children have brown eyes.
Fact 3: Half of the children are girls.

If the first three statements are facts, which of the following statements must also be a fact?
I: At least one girl has blue eyes.
II:  To of the children are boys.
III:The boys have brown eyes.

| A: | I only | B: | II only |
|---|---|---|---|
| C: | II and III only | D: | None of the statements is a known fact. |

**3.**
Fact 1:Most stuffed toys are stuffed with cotton.
Fact 2:There are stuffed bears and stuffed lions.
Fact 3:Some sofas are stuffed with cotton.

If the first three statements are facts, which of the following
statements must also be a fact?
I:Only children's sofa are stuffed with cotton.
II:All stuffed lions are stuffed with cotton.
III:Stuffed monkeys are not stuffed with cotton.

| A:   I only | B:   II only |
|---|---|
| C:   II and III only | D:   None of the statements is a known fact. |

**4.**
Fact 1:Maryln said, "Anny and I both have cats."
Fact 2:Anny said, "I don't have a cat."
Fact 3:Maryln always tells the truth, but Anny sometimes lies.

If the first three statements are facts, which of the following
statements must also be a fact?
I:Anny has a cat.
II:Maryln has a cat.
III:Anny is lying.

| A:   I only | B:   II only |
|---|---|
| C:   II and III only | D:   None of the statements is a known fact. |

5.
Fact 1:Rob has four vehicles.
Fact 2:Two of the vehicles are Blue.
Fact 3:One of the vehicles is a minivan.

If the first three statements are facts, which of the following
statements must also be a fact?
I:Rob has a red minivan.
II:Rob has three cars.
III:Rob's favorite color is Blue.

| A: | I only | B: | II only |
|---|---|---|---|
| C: | II and III only | D: | None of the statements is a known fact. |

# ANSWER

## Unit 1: Pattern completion
1) D
2) D
3) D
4) A
5) D
6) B
7) B
8) B
9) C
10) D

## Unit 2: Serial Reasoning
1) A
2) B
3) B
4) A
5) B
6) C
7) E
8) C
9) C
10) C

## Unit 3: spatial visualization
1) D
2) D
3) C
4) B
5) D
6) D
7) B
8) A
9) B
10) D

## Unit 4: Reasoning by analogy
1) A
2) D
3) A
4) C
5) B
6) C
7) C
8) C
9) B
10) A

## Unit 5: Sequence completion by analogy
1) C
2) C
3) A
4) C
5) D
6) D
7) B
8) D
9) A
10) A

## Unit 6: Logical reasoning
Section 1
1) 5
2) 6
3) 2
4) 2
5) 3
6) 6
7) 3
8) 18

## Unit 6: Logical reasoning
Section 2
1)   17
2)   3
3)   25
4)   25
5)   30

## Unit 6: Logical reasoning
Section 5
1)   8
2)   9
3)   5
4)   5
5)   11
6)   9

## Unit 6: Logical reasoning
Section 3
1)   3
2)   3
3)   2
4)   1
5)   2
6)   1
7)   2
8)   1

## Unit 7 : Visual Recognition
1)   A
2)   A
3)   C
4)   C
5)   C
6)   C
7)   A
8)   D
9)   A
10)  C

## Unit 6: Logical reasoning
Section 4
1)   1,33,4,5,7,88
2)   1,7
3)   1,88
4)   1,4,5,66,7,88
5)   1
6)   2
7)   2,3
8)   2,4

## Unit 8 Logical thinking word problems
1)   B
2)   B
3)   D
4)   D
5)   D

## TEACHERS TIPS

**Critical thinking is important aspect of elementary education but its not easy to train kids in that area**

Critical thinking skills are not only applicable to subjects like science and math, but also vital for success in all subject areas, and everyday life as well.

**A few techniques to encourage critical thinking are:**

1. Ask questions.
2. Use analogies to explain.
3. Promote interaction among students.
4. Encourage decision-making.
5. Ask open-ended questions.
6. Allow reflection time.
7. Use real-life problems.
8. Allow for thinking practice.
9. Brainstorming with a group of kids.
10. Playing sorting games and Puzzles.

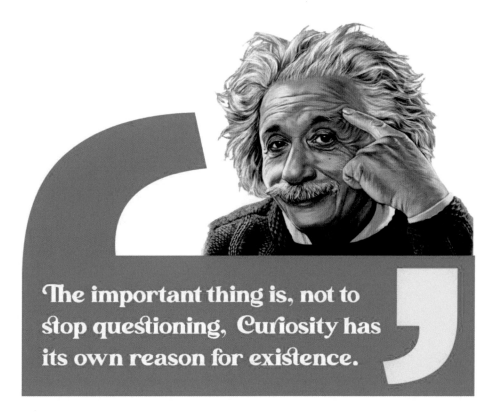

The important thing is, not to stop questioning, Curiosity has its own reason for existence.

Made in the USA
Middletown, DE
04 October 2024

62018736R00022